P9-EDK-335

ALL KINDS OF MONEY

ALL KINDS OF MONEY

A MONEY POWER BOOK

by DAVID A. ADLER

illustrations by Tom Huffman

Franklin Watts
New York / London / Toronto / Sydney
1984

To Michelle, Shayna, and Elliot

R.L. 2.8 Spache Revised Formula

Library of Congress Cataloging in Publication Data

Adler, David A.
  All kinds of money.

  (A Money power book)
  Summary: Discusses the history of money from
the mediums of exchange used by primitive
societies to the currency, and variations thereof,
used in today's highly complex world.
  1. Money—Juvenile literature. [1. Money] I.
Huffman, Tom, ill. II. Title. III. Series.
HG221.5.A34 1984   332.4   84-2190
ISBN 0-531-04627-3

If you want to buy apples, a shirt, shoes, or a book, you need money. If you want to see a movie or take a train ride, you need money too.

5

You know what money looks like. Each
country has its own. In the United States people
spend dollars and cents. In Great Britain they
spend pounds and pence. The French spend francs
and centimes. Italians spend lire and centesimi.
Mexicans spend pesos and centavos. And
Russians spend rubles and kopeks.

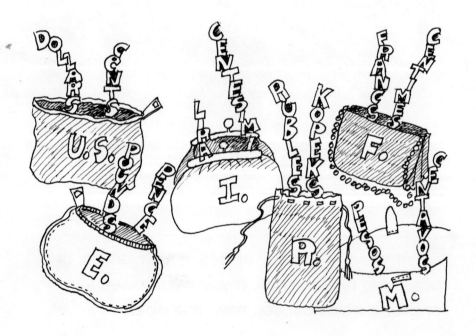

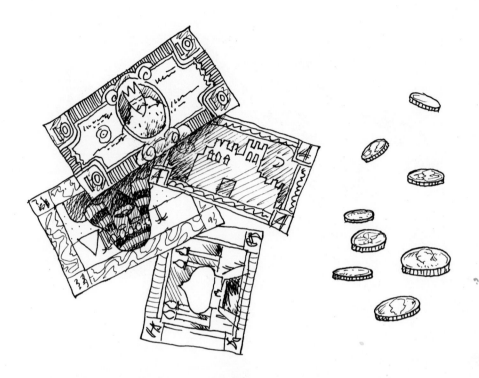

Paper money has pictures on it, pictures of
buildings, presidents, kings, and queens. Coins are
usually round and made of metal. At one time,
coins were mostly made of gold and silver, metals
which have their own value. But today most coins
are made of alloys. Alloys are mixtures of cheaper
metals such as copper, zinc, and nickel.

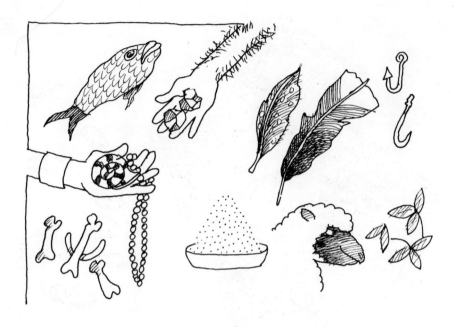

But money wasn't always made of paper or metal. Shells, dried fish, salt, and pigs' bones were once used as money. Sheep, fishhooks, feathers, beads, tea, and rocks were once money, too. And before all those things were used as money, there was a time when there was no money at all.

8

There was no money thousands of years ago because people didn't need it. People were **self-sufficient.** They didn't depend on others for the things they needed. If people were hungry, they gathered their own food. If they wanted meat, they hunted and killed an animal. They did everything themselves. They didn't buy things from other people, so they didn't need money.

But some people liked to hunt. Others were
better at making clubs or clothes, or gathering
berries and other foods. Of course a hunter still
needed clothes. And someone who gathered food
still wanted meat. So people traded. The hunter
traded animals for berries, clubs, and clothes. The
club-maker traded clubs for berries, clothes, and
animals.

10

A system of trading one thing for another is called **barter.** In many parts of Africa and Asia people still barter. Children often barter, too. When a child trades a few marbles for some crayons or an apple for some cookies, that's barter.

But barter is not a perfect system. It can cause problems. How many cookies is one apple worth? And when hunters traded animals for berries, how would they know how many berries one animal was worth? What if the hunter didn't want all those berries? What if the hunter didn't want any berries?

Hunters might be willing to trade an animal for some berries if they knew that they could trade the berries for something they *did* want. They might trade an animal for some berries and then trade the berries for a club.

13

If people would all be willing to trade for berries, then you could use a bucket of berries to buy whatever you needed. Berries would be a kind of money. But they wouldn't be a very good kind of money. Berries spoil. If berries were money and you saved a bucket of them, within a short while you would have a bucket of "spoiled" money.

One of the first kinds of money wasn't much better than berries. It ate grass and had to be fenced in so that the "money" wouldn't run away. The money was sheep. Sheep gave wool and so everyone wanted them. But sheep didn't make very good money. Sheep could die and no one wanted "dead" money. And if something cost just half a sheep, you couldn't cut a live sheep in half to pay for it.

15

Salt was used as money, too. But salt can be washed away in the rain.

Rocks were used as money, but they were too heavy to carry around.

Feathers were used as money, but they could easily be blown away.

Fishhooks were also once used as money, but why would anyone who didn't live near the water want a fishhook?

What would make good money?

Centuries ago people found that certain metals, such as gold and silver, made good money. The amount of gold and silver available was limited, so the metals had value. But there was still enough around to make money. Metals can be cut into small pieces and it's easy to tell how much each piece is worth. Just weigh it. The more it weighs, the more it's worth.

Gold and silver had other advantages. Sheep have to be fed. Gold and silver don't. Salt can wash away in the rain. Gold and silver can't.

At first, the pieces of gold and silver that were used as money came in all different sizes. Then coins were made. Each coin had a certain weight. That saved people time. Coins didn't have to be weighed each time something was bought or sold. People knew what they weighed and what they were worth.

Gold was used as money in many places. So
was silver. People were happy to be paid with gold
or silver coins because they knew that they could
use the coins to buy whatever they wanted.

But a great many coins are heavy. Carrying them around was difficult. So paper money was invented.

The first paper money was a printed promise. It was a promise that the money could be traded for gold or silver coins.

People were happy to be paid with paper money because they knew that they could buy things with it. They also knew that they could exchange the paper money for gold or silver coins.

There was a time when you could take paper money to a bank and say, "I want a gold coin," or "I want a silver dollar." There were still gold and silver coins and the bank would exchange your paper money for those coins. You can't do that anymore. The United States and most other countries no longer make gold and silver coins.

But you can buy gold or silver with paper
money. You can take the paper money to a jeweler
and use it to buy gold and silver jewelry. There are
also gold and silver coins that are still being made.
But these are not used as money.

People buy gold and silver because they believe these precious metals will not lose their value. If you have a certain amount of paper money and prices go up, you cannot buy as much with the paper money. When this happens it is known as **inflation.** The money is slowly losing some of its value.

24

Many of the people buying gold and silver today feel that as the prices of televisions, food, cars, and other items go up, the price of gold and silver will go up, too. It will keep its value. But, of course, that's not always true. Even in times of inflation, the prices of gold and silver do not always go up.

The real value of paper money doesn't come from the gold and silver it can buy. You can take paper money to a supermarket and buy milk, bread, cheese, ice cream, or meat. You can buy a shirt, shoes, pants, or a coat with paper money. People are happy to trade things for money, because they know that they can use the money to buy just about anything.

Dollars, cents, pounds, pence, francs, centimes, rubles, and kopeks are one kind of money, the kind issued by different governments. They're called **currency.**

Most working people aren't paid with currency. They're paid with a different kind of money. They're paid by **check.** Millions of checks are written every day. Someone who writes a check is telling a bank to give a certain amount of his or her money to someone else. Since checks can be used to buy things, they are a kind of money.

In many places—in department stores, hotels, and restaurants—people use **credit cards.** Since credit cards are used to pay for things, they are also a kind of money.

It's hard to imagine a world without money. Money is used to express the value, the price of an item, that is being sold. It's used to pay for things that we buy. It is also used to pay people who do work for us. And money can be saved.

In today's world, people have jobs that require very special skills. We have astronauts, lifeguards, automobile designers, animal trainers, and dairy farmers. It's almost impossible to imagine these people, or just about anyone, being able to trade their skills for all the things they need.

What would an astronaut trade for a loaf of bread? Astronauts pilot spacecraft and bakers don't own spacecraft. Astronauts wouldn't be able to trade their skills for a loaf of bread.

What would a lifeguard trade for a pair of shoes? Unless the shoemaker owned a pool, or lived on the beach, he or she wouldn't need to trade with a lifeguard. But a lifeguard would still need shoes!

With money, astronauts can use some of the money they are paid to buy bread. Lifeguards can spend the money they earn to buy shoes.

We need money. We need it because we're no longer self-sufficient. We need other people. We need doctors to keep us healthy, bakers to bake our bread, and builders to build our homes. We need money because we need to buy the things other people make, and we need to pay for the work that other people do for us.